R.M. HEDGCOTH

FINDING CALM AMIDST
COVID-19
PANIC

Lilac Center

ISBN: 978-0-9962112-5-3
Copyright © SunStar Books

CONTENTS

About The Lilac Center 04

Preface 04

What Exactly is DBT?...06

Committing to LIFE 09

Accepting What Is 12

Willing or Willful? 16

Be Present 21

How To Be Mindful 25

Relax. Refuel. Repeat...33

COVID-19 Self-Care Kit.......................................36

ABOUT THE LILAC CENTER

Lilac Center

The Lilac Center is based in Kansas City, Missouri. Led by Director Amy Tibbitts, LSCSW, the Lilac Center serves clients of all ages through individual therapy, group therapy, intensive outpatient programs, and more.

Amy and her trained staff of therapists have been providing Dialectical Behavioral Therapy (DBT) in a private practice setting since October of 2000. The Lilac Center professionals have extensive knowledge and experience in treating Borderline Personality Disorder (BPD).

Delivered through a fundamental core of compassion, strength, and sensitivity, the Lilac Center's approach to therapy is based upon DBT principles of mindfulness, distress tolerance, interpersonal effectiveness, and emotion regulation.

Learn more at *www.lilaccenter.org*.

PREFACE

No matter where you turn, life may feel utterly chaotic right now. Maybe even foreign. Some say it even feels a little like the Twilight Zone. Or a crazy horror story. The comparisons are endless.

Graduation plans. Family get-togethers. Eating out in restaurants. Masks. Medical appointments. Social interactions. School routines. Grocery shopping. Employment demands. Increased isolation. Job lay-offs.

The list of the ways our lives have been impacted by COVID-19 goes on forever.

As we all navigate this "new normal" that is taking shape in a world dominated by COVID-19, collective questions, fears, and worries abound.

At the Lilac Center, we get it. And we want you to know your feelings are completely understandable.

Rest assured we are here to help.

While there is no magic wand to wave all the uncertainty away, there are specific skills and tools to help you make every day your best day, or at the very least, better.

Maybe you are considering therapy or are currently seeing a therapist. While we believe that working with a trained mental health professional is the optimal choice, we understand that this is not always possible due to practitioner availability, time, distance, work schedules, or financial constraints.

But no matter your present situation, our goal with this book is to provide tools based on dialectical behavior therapy (DBT) that you can use to help manage your emotions in stressful situations, such as the current pandemic, and ultimately improve your well-being.

We may not be magicians, but we do know that the *power of thought* can be truly magical.

"THAT WAS HER MAGIC. SHE COULD STILL SEE THE SUNSET, EVEN ON THOSE DARKEST DAYS."

— *Atticus*

WHAT EXACTLY IS DBT?

DBT = Dialectical Behavior Therapy.

If the term "dialectical" is new to you, no worries.

In simplest terms, "dialectical" is defined as "a synthesis or integration of opposites" by DBT creator, Marsha Linehan, PhD, ABPP.

In the late 1980s, Linehan, an American psychologist, author, and founder of Seattle-based Behavioral Tech, created dialectical behavior therapy (DBT) based upon the philosophy that there can be balance between two contradictory extremes.

Dialectics play an important role in DBT because it suggests that the fusion of acceptance and change is not only possible, but also critical to long-term success when it comes to emotional control.

In other words, DBT can help us accept the reality of what is, while also acknowledging that change is necessary and possible.

Here are a few examples of dialectical situations:

- When we are angry with someone but still love that person very much.
- When we want to do something perfectly but keep making mistakes.
- When we are painfully honest with someone while speaking in a gentle way.

Our lives are filled with opposites, and while many things are indeed contradictory, they can both be true ... at the same time!

This is the essence of dialectics.

This is a critical component of DBT strategies which adhere to the practice of validating feelings, experiences, and beliefs, while also asserting that change is critical to a person's path forward.

It is through dialectical practices that we can find common ground between thought extremes. Rather than simply being driven by all-or-nothing, black-and-white thinking, we can learn that opposites can coexist.

DBT will encourage healthy relationships and interactions by helping you to understand that truth can lie in a variety of perspectives.

Applying dialectical principles to your everyday thought processes, conversations, personal and professional interactions, and relationships will help spur positive change, conflict resolution, and conscientious communication.

It can also play a significant role in weathering trying times such as those brought about by the COVID-19 pandemic.

In life, there is one true constant ... and that is change.

Accepting that change is inevitable — while also admitting that

there are steps we can always take to improve our situations —
represents dialectics at its best.

When it comes to the coronavirus and COVID-19, news headlines,
personal stories, and many unknowns may bring us daily anxiety,
but there are skills we can use to alter our reactions to life's
unpredictable developments.

"YOU ARE THE SKY. EVERYTHING ELSE – IT'S JUST THE WEATHER."

— Pema Chödrön, Buddhist teacher, author, nun, and mother

WORDS TO REPEAT:
I can find common ground between
opposing extremes.

COMMITTING TO LIFE

DBT has helped so many people gain a fresh outlook on life, and it can help you during these unprecedented times.

A comprehensive and practical approach to managing emotions and changing behaviors, DBT is founded upon four behavior skill modules of mindfulness, distress tolerance, interpersonal effectiveness, and emotion regulation and fuses acceptance-oriented skills with change-oriented skills.

However, for DBT to be successful, there is one critical caveat.

The underlying assumption is that DBT will be ineffective if the client is not alive or refuses to attend treatment sessions.
To that end, to successfully incorporate DBT skills, you *must* commit to life.

This is essential.

You must also have patience and be willing to take time to learn the skills, understand them, and apply these principles to everyday living.

DBT is backed by years of studies proving that this evidence-based treatment truly does change lives. It works because it targets the catalyst behind dangerous and maladaptive behaviors while also providing skills that are instrumental in changing how you process emotions and react to life's curveballs.

Perhaps during this difficult time, you have depressive episodes or have thoughts of self-harm. Maybe you feel isolated, lonely, and have increased feelings of stress and anxiety.

According to the Centers for Disease Control (CDC), an infectious disease outbreak can cause the following:

- Fear and worry about your own health and the health of your loved ones, your financial situation or job, or loss of support services you rely on
- Changes in sleep or eating patterns
- Difficulty sleeping or concentrating
- Worsening of chronic health problems
- Worsening of mental health conditions
- Increased use of tobacco and/or alcohol and other substances

You might have other circumstances in your life that are also compounding your stress during this time.

Perhaps you are a frontline worker, are caring for a loved one at home, have an underlying health condition or an existing mental illness. Even in the absence of ancillary issues, it is perfectly normal and understandable to experience stress during a global pandemic such as what we are seeing with the new coronavirus.

The good news is that you absolutely possess the power to take charge of your emotional health and make positive changes. Better days are within your reach.

"KEEP YOUR FACE TO THE SUN AND YOU WILL NEVER SEE THE SHADOWS."

— Helen Keller

WORDS TO REPEAT:
I choose life. Always.

ACCEPTING WHAT IS

One of the first steps on a proactive path forward to improved mental balance is this: ACCEPT.

Wait, accept what? Accept that the coronavirus makes life feel out of control right now? Accept that I can't do what I want to do when I want to do it? Accept that I need to wear a mask much of the time? Accept that I can't see my family and friends? Accept that life-as-usual seems to be in the rearview mirror (at least for the moment)? Accept that my professional world has dramatically changed? Accept that a barrage of frightening news fills my phone, TV, and radio every day? Accept that schools are in uncharted territory? Accept that I lost my job or got laid off?

In short, yes.

You must accept all that … and more.

Here's the twist: Do you have to *like* all these things? Absolutely not. Do you have to *approve* of these things? No. Must you *resign* yourself to being miserable every day? Definitely not.

The key to navigating these thoughts is a practice, or skill, known as RADICAL ACCEPTANCE.

And while this may sound like something easy to do, it can be harder than you might think. It takes a lot of practice and patience to master.

The truth of the matter is this: As the old Buddhist saying goes, *"pain is inevitable, but suffering is optional."*

We all know life is not perfect. And life hurts, whether we like it or not. But not letting go of pain can make us feel needlessly worse.

If you fight reality and *what is*, you are certain to feel worse and worse. In fact, fighting reality is truly exhausting. And it is pointless.

Because you cannot change what *is*.

But once you fully accept reality for what it is, then you can begin to make changes in how you react to that reality and ultimately ease your suffering by changing your perspective.

During the coronavirus pandemic, you likely feel an array of emotions, most of which probably are not joyful or positive.

Perhaps you feel cheated out of your high school graduation or your high school prom; perhaps you didn't get to take the dream vacation you had planned; perhaps your employer had to close down and you lost your job. Maybe you even had to call off an important celebration or life event.

There are an infinite number of ways that nearly everyone has been negatively impacted in one way or another during this global pandemic.

And that reality cannot be changed.

But you can repeat these words to yourself:

"I am in this situation. I do not like it. I am not happy about it. But it is what it is and there's nothing I can do about it."

Once you radically accept something, you will ultimately give yourself the freedom to let go of pain to make more room in your mind and heart for happier and healthier thoughts.

Again, to reiterate, acceptance does not mean you have to love what is happening. But when you accept reality for what it is, and understand that you cannot change what is, you can then turn your energies to more positive pursuits.

Coronavirus has changed our world. That is a fact.

It is a safe bet that most of us do not like many of the ways our lives have changed.

But once we accept that this is what it is, we can untangle ourselves from distressing thoughts that may consume our days and subsequently rob us of joy in our lives.

Remember that radical acceptance takes practice. Give yourself time to perfect this skill. Start with small things such as red lights on a drive, long lines in a store, or a rainstorm that you never expected.

Accepting the small things in life will help you tremendously when much bigger, more difficult situations come up.

While we cannot avoid pain in our lives, we can adjust how we respond to it and how much we suffer from it.

Take a breath, accept what is, and move on.

You *will* get through this.

"FOR AFTER ALL, THE BEST THING ONE CAN DO WHEN IT IS RAINING IS LET IT RAIN."

— *Henry Wadsworth Longfellow*

WORDS TO REPEAT:
I can accept circumstances without judgment.

WILLING OR WILLFUL?

Once you have accepted that life is what it is, you can move on to change.

But first you will have to ask yourself, "Am I *willing* ... or am I *willful*?" This is an important question that should be considered with honest introspection.

To be willing is to be open and to accept that, sometimes, difficult steps must be taken to move forward or improve a situation. Willingness also requires putting aside our own needs, desires, and agendas.

When we are willing, we can more effectively connect with the world around us which will enable us to handle anxiety and problem-solve in more efficient ways.

During the pandemic, once we have accepted that there isn't anything we can to do to change what's happening around us personally, locally, and globally, we can then focus on making changes to improve our own individual situation and our emotional mindset.

What does that look like?

Here is one example.

During the current global COVID-19 pandemic, we are all being asked to wear masks to help slow the spread of the virus.

Some people are completely fine with this request because they understand and appreciate the science and rationale behind it.

Others feel strongly that this request translates into an infringement on personal freedom.

So, are you willing to comply and take precautions to help not only yourself, but others also, and wear a mask?

Or do you take a willful stance, and argue that no one has any right to tell you what to do and thus refuse to wear a mask?

This is a situation where dialectics, or two opposing forces, are at play.

You may not necessarily *want* to wear a mask, but perhaps you do it anyway knowing it comes at the urging from the nation's top infectious disease experts.

On the flip side, if you choose not to wear mask, perhaps there are other ways you can still help to curb the virus spread while adhering to your wishes for personal freedom.

While the best option is to comply with medical advice, you can still find small ways to adopt a position of willingness even while you are choosing to willfully refuse to follow mask mandates. In doing

so, you will be taking steps to move toward a more willing mindset. For example:

- You could stay home and dramatically limit your time outside of your residence.
- If you are not wearing a mask, you could make sure that you socially distance when you are outdoors in a public setting around people.
- You could do your best to think of others, be considerate, and understand that while something like wearing a seatbelt is more about personal safety measures, mask-wearing is more about keeping others around you safe from a virus that you may unknowingly be carrying.

The current pandemic has created an environment where you must reconcile what you *want* to do with what you *should* do per medical experts' advice, which is to wear a properly fitting mask in public settings to help keep yourself and others around you safe from virus transmission.

Because there are many people who do not want to wear masks for various reasons, this may cause other mask-wearers to feel tremendous anger, anxiety — or both! — when they see others not following those protocols.

This is another situation in which a little flexibility in thinking can go a long way.

Using the radical acceptance skill, we can acknowledge that we cannot control others' actions. Again, this does not mean we have to *like* that we cannot control others, but we need to understand that this is simply how it is.

While we cannot control what others do, what *can* we control?

If you are thinking, "*I can control what I do*," you are already in the right train of thought.

Here are some ways you can take control of your personal safety:

- You can wear your mask.
- You can maintain a safe distance from people.
- You can wash your hands frequently and use your hand sanitizer.
- You can even wear gloves if you wish.
- You can limit your exposure to outside places and people.
- You can avoid groups of 10 or more people.

The point is, while you may not particularly like or enjoy a specific situation — albeit a grocery store where not everyone is wearing their masks properly or a park where not everyone is adhering to social distancing — *you* can change how you react to those situations.

At the end of the day, you can feel confident that you have done everything in your power to keep yourself safe, even if others around you are not necessarily doing the same thing.

Willingness is letting go of what you cannot control and accepting what you *can* control.

When you are willing to adapt to fluid situations, you will find this will help you cope much more effectively with life's curveballs than if you choose to be intolerant, willful, and fight circumstances around you.

It takes much less effort to go *with* the grain than against it.

In the big picture, controlling the spread of the coronavirus requires a collective effort to put others before ourselves and to do what is best for the community as a whole, even if it means being a little uncomfortable, inconvenienced, or feeling constitutionally stifled.

"YOU MUST BE SHAPELESS, FORMLESS, LIKE WATER. WHEN YOU POUR WATER IN A CUP, IT BECOMES THE CUP. WHEN YOU POUR WATER IN A BOTTLE, IT BECOMES THE BOTTLE. WHEN YOU POUR WATER IN A TEAPOT, IT BECOMES THE TEAPOT. WATER CAN DRIP AND IT CAN CRASH. BECOME LIKE WATER, MY FRIEND."

— *Bruce Lee*

WORDS TO REPEAT:
I can be open to change.

BE PRESENT

We have covered a lot of ground in a short amount of time thus far.

You have learned what dialectics are. You have come to understand why radical acceptance is so important in controlling your emotions. And you have learned how willingness plays an important role in your ability to make positive changes.

This brings us to the very centerpiece of DBT: MINDFULNESS.

During this time of tremendous upheaval in our lives, we have a prime opportunity to tap into the remarkable power of mindfulness.

If you believe that mindfulness means "paying attention," you would be correct. However, there is so much more that makes up this amazing philosophy.

You might be tempted to think, "Mindfulness is not really for me."

But if you are experiencing feelings such as:

- Irritability
- Inability to focus
- Lack of patience
- Difficulty sleeping
- Rushing through life
- Constantly distracted
- Worrying about the future
- Feeling compelled to multitask
- Overthinking everything
- Persistent exhaustion

... then perhaps you could benefit from a little mindfulness in your life.

Practicing mindfulness will allow you to expand your awareness, develop increased tolerance for strong emotions, and see situations with fresh clarity.

Evaluating your feelings and behaviors without judgment will reveal patterns in thought triggers more clearly. This improved understanding will enable you to rein in impulsive thoughts and actions, especially when it comes to excessive worry, stress, and fear related to the coronavirus pandemic.

Consider all the ways that science has proven how mindfulness can impact us physically and mentally.

Mindfulness can ...

- Help relieve stress
- Improve sleep
- Reduce anxiety
- Help prevent depression
- Increase overall well-being
- Lessen emotional reactivity
- Lower blood pressure
- Increase self-awareness
- Enhance focus and productivity
- Boost memory

What's not to love? Why not give mindfulness a try?

It will not only help you during this unsettling time, but in all aspects of your life, as well.

How exactly can mindfulness help you cope with the current pandemic?

For one thing, mindfulness will keep you rooted in the present.

That is not to say that we can or must be "in the present" every minute of the day ... that is simply not reasonable to expect.

Our mind wanders, our thoughts drift, our focus can change at the drop of a hat. We are human; that is how we are wired. However, try being intentionally mindful for just a few minutes several times a day. The more you do this, the more your brain will start to embrace this way of thinking.

By using mindfulness, we can shift our thoughts away from distressing anxiety over looming uncertainty and constant mental chatter to return to the here and now present moment. And in this moment, we can tell ourselves that we are, in fact, ok.

The truth is that worrying over what we cannot control will not change the outcome of anything. We cannot change how long the pandemic will last, how others around us behave, or how our immediate surroundings will be impacted.

Therefore, we must make peace with the fact that we have uncertainty in our lives. Even if the pandemic were not happening, our lives are full of other uncertainties ranging from health issues, professional endeavors, educational pursuits, relationships, and so much more.

While making peace with all this uncertainty might seem easier said than done, it is possible with intentional and deliberate thought processes which will, in turn, help build better coping skills.

And at the end of the day, that is what we are all doing: coping with this new world created by the coronavirus pandemic.

Using mindfulness, we can learn to recognize what we are feeling while at the same time learn to let go of anxiety so we can avoid getting stuck in repetitive loops of negative thoughts.

Doing this will allow us to *respond* to things we feel rather than *react* and assist us in finding more effective solutions to worrisome thoughts that may be consuming us during these challenging times.

Ultimately, practicing mindfulness will grant us the time, energy, and capacity to calm our inner turmoil and reconnect with joy and contentment.

"TRUST THE WAIT. EMBRACE THE UNCERTAINTY. ENJOY THE BEAUTY OF BECOMING. WHEN NOTHING IS CERTAIN, ANYTHING IS POSSIBLE."

— *Mandy Hale*

WORDS TO REPEAT:
I can be present in this moment.

HOW TO BE MINDFUL

Perhaps now you are saying to yourself, "Ok, this all sounds pretty good. How exactly can I be more mindful?"

The beautiful thing about mindfulness is that it is not complicated and there really is no one right way to practice it.

It is more about discovering what works for you and finding ways to be present in your life and engaged with your surroundings.

We are all reinventing our lives to some degree or another during this pandemic. We are staying home more, we may be homeschooling our kids, and we may be working from home. We are navigating a whole new set of restrictions and rules.

Things have changed; life as we knew it has been fundamentally altered and no one can say when things might return to our definition of "normal."

The good news is, there are countless ways to cultivate heightened focus, increase productivity, and enhance life satisfaction with mindfulness strategies — during COVID-19 times and beyond.

Here are five ways you can practice mindfulness:

S.T.O.P

When you feel overwhelmed by incessant news reports, anxious about going out in public, or worried you might get sick, here is one skill you can use: S.T.O.P.

S – Stop.
T – Take a breath.
O – Observe what is going on.
P – Proceed.

Developed by Jon Kabat-Zinn, a prominent mindfulness researcher, this relatively simple skill can be practiced anytime, anywhere.

The more times you do this during the day, the more you will refine your ability to quiet the busyness of your mind and become more fully in tune with your surroundings, thoughts, feelings, and behaviors.

BREATHE

One of the easiest ways you can redirect your attention to the present moment is by noticing your breath.

You may have found that when you are anxious or stressed, your breathing becomes rapid and shallow. This is part of the fight-or-flight response. This type of breathing increases our oxygen levels to prepare us to take any necessary action.

However, if we do not need to take any action, then this leads to a temporary imbalance of oxygen and carbon dioxide in our body which can aggravate feelings of anxiety and stress.

By controlling your breathing, you can help to improve some of these symptoms brought on by excessively rapid, shallow breathing, or hyperventilation.

Try this:

Simply focus on breathing in ... and out. Breathe in deeply through your nose clear to your diaphragm and count to one on the inhale. Then briefly pause, and slowly exhale through your nose on two.
Hear these words in your mind as you breathe:

"I breathe in peace."
"I exhale stress."

You can repeat this sequence for several minutes while keeping your mind focused on your breathing and your counting.

This simple and elemental act of very deep, slow breathing has been shown to calm the autonomic nervous system which is responsible for regulating involuntary body functions such as heartbeat, blood flow, breathing, and digestion.

It is important to remember that while symptoms of hyperventilation are very real and often unpleasant, they are not usually life-threatening.

By slowing down your breath, carbon dioxide will build up in the blood, which stimulates the response of the vagus nerve and triggers the body's balancing capabilities. This will induce feelings of calm throughout the body.

Know that relief can be found through regular breathing and relaxation techniques, such as those listed above.

PAY ATTENTION

Living life on autopilot is something we are probably all familiar with. It is so easy to get caught up in daily routines, to do the same things over and over, and to mentally "check out."

The problem with "checking out" is that it has many detrimental effects on our well-being.

It robs us of creativity and innovation if we are simply doing the same routine every day. It inhibits our energy level because we are not engaged or connected to whatever we are doing.

Checking out also takes a toll on our moods and relationships, because we may be emotionally detached or even plagued by feelings of inadequacy.

Instead, try "checking in" several times a day.

Whether you are cooking dinner, driving home, taking a shower, or helping your child with homework, be present in the moment.

If you are taking a walk, notice how the breeze blows, how leaves may be changing colors, or how flowers are blooming. Notice cloud formations, a scent that lingers in the air, flights of insects, or the chatter of birds.

If you are in the car, office, classroom, or a waiting room, observe your surroundings conscientiously and focus for several minutes on a certain item.

When we allow ourselves to simply observe what we are experiencing without reacting to it, judging it, resisting it, or hanging on to it, the world will feel a little slower, a little less chaotic, and a little more under control.

ONE THING

While we may feel as though we are being especially productive if we are multitasking, odds are good we are not.

Research studies have repeatedly shown that multitasking is less productive than if you were to do one single thing at a time.

Why is this?

The answer is quite logical. When we multitask, our efficiency and performance are compromised because our brain — no matter how amazing and powerful it is! — cannot effectively and fully focus on more than one thing at a time.

In fact, it's more likely that multitasking is slowing you down, leading to mistakes, and ultimately, stressing you out.

Consider these actions: walking while you are texting, answering an email while someone is talking to you, working on two projects simultaneously, driving your car while reprimanding a child in the back seat. The list goes on and on of all the ways we may multitask on any given day.

But studies have shown that we are much more efficient and successful when we focus our energies on one task at hand. Here is a little acronym to help you avoid multitasking:

F.O.C.U.S. – Follow One Course Until Successful

Created by American businessman and author Robert T. Kiyosaki, this little gem goes hand in hand with mindfulness principles, as it can remind you to respond to one thing in life now, today, in this moment.

Be selective and deliberate about what you choose to focus your attention on. This principle can be applied to so many things in life and can help you prioritize tasks and ultimately perform them more effectively and mindfully.

While it can be challenging to function effectively and efficiently in stressful situations such as when we are being bombarded by frightening media, training our mind to focus on one thing at a time can improve concentration as well as our ability to tune out background noise around us.

CULTIVATE CONTENTMENT

During this time of alarming headlines, rising COVID-19 cases, global unrest, and ongoing uncertainty, it is easy to lose sight of the good in our life.

But as the old saying goes, every morning that we open our eyes is a gift. And as we become more aware of the big and small moments in our lives, we will, in turn, become more grateful.

Embracing gratitude in small ways every day will help us to weather the more trying times such as those we are currently facing. It can also improve our health.

Research has shown that mindfully practicing gratitude can benefit us through:

- Improved energy levels
- Better sleep
- Lower blood pressure
- Reduced symptoms of depression and increased optimism
- Enhanced sensitivity and empathy

Being grateful can also brighten our days when we feel particularly lonely or isolated — a very commonly reported consequence of social distancing and staying home during this historic pandemic. While it's true that finding joy may take a little more effort on some days, remember there is always light to be found.

One way to increase positive thoughts is with a gratitude journal.

At the start of the day or just before bed, jot down one, two, or three things you are grateful for. You could do this on a daily or weekly basis. Make this a habit and before long, you will reap the rewards of a

grateful heart and mind.

Above all, gratitude breeds more gratitude. And the happier we are, the more positive feelings we will have and the more distracted we will be from things in our lives that may be troubling us.

Take a moment to think about some things that make your heart happy.

It could be something as simple as a beautiful flower, a favorite song, a cherished memory, or something more personally impactful such as healthcare providers, a beloved family member or friend, or a spiritual higher power.

Feeling scared and overwhelmed during these unfamiliar times is perfectly normal and acceptable. But the simple act of gratitude can help offset the stress and worry that may blanket you during these unprecedented times.

Finding joy every single day may sometimes be challenging. And that is ok. You must grant yourself grace while accepting and embracing all your feelings — good and bad — without judgment.

It is important to understand that gratitude will not remove negative or painful experiences from our lives. For example, it will not necessarily lessen sadness over losing a loved one.

But, combined with mindfulness, gratitude can help us persevere through challenging times by bringing the good and positive elements of our lives into sharper focus.

Fuel gratitude by ...

- Writing a thank-you note
- Saying a few kind words to someone
- Posting a positive review for a product or service

- Taking time to appreciate nature
- Not speaking negatively about other people
- Calling a loved one
- Offering to help someone in some way
- Performing a random act of kindness
- Giving yourself the gift of time to do something you love
- Donating clothing to a homeless shelter or charity

It is easy to get caught up in the rush of life and dismiss all the things we should be thankful for.

Devote a little time each day to acknowledge what you are grateful for. By nurturing your own happiness, you will subsequently increase the happiness of others, as well.

Gratitude is truly the gift that keeps on giving.

"FEELING GRATITUDE AND NOT EXPRESSING IT IS LIKE WRAPPING A PRESENT AND NOT GIVING IT."

— *William Arthur Ward*

WORDS TO REPEAT:
I can be mindful and grateful.

RELAX. REFUEL. REPEAT.

At this point, you should take a moment and give yourself a little pat on the back.

While you may be stressed out, confused, and anxious about living during these unpredictable pandemic times, you have already taken steps to do something about it. By reading this book and taking time to understand the DBT concepts presented, you have equipped yourself with tools to take stronger emotional control over your life.

- You now understand that to make positive changes, you must start by RADICALLY ACCEPTING — without judgment — circumstances that you cannot control.
- You also understand how WILLINGNESS, rather than WILLFULNESS, can dramatically enhance your ability to respond to challenging times.
- Further, you have been shown how MINDFULNESS and GRATITUDE can empower your days on so many levels.

What happens now?

You keep going. You move on. You put one foot in front of the other.

Even though we are all living life in this strange new world where jobs may still be disrupted, schools are charting new paths, health may be compromised, and social distancing is still advised, it is possible to tackle difficult emotions and rise above these challenging times.

Stressful days no doubt still lie ahead, but you can now better understand your feelings, evaluate your thoughts, and, in turn, respond more effectively to situations you may face.

And while the strategies outlined in this book may sound like small steps to take, when practiced consistently, they can result in big, positive changes over time.

At the end of the day, you must care for yourself and your own well-being before you can care for anyone else who may need you. Self-care is critical and necessary anytime, but especially during this unique time in human history.

Take time to take care of YOU, give yourself grace, and remember to breathe. Think about how you have handled uncertainty in the past and draw upon those activities, thoughts, people, or places that have helped you navigate difficult times behind you.

Additionally, try incorporating some of these simple techniques in your day to improve your well-being:

- Take a break from the news.
- Give yourself some space — literally. Go outdoors for a short walk. Move around.
- Slow down, take a step back, and reevaluate your situation.
- Set goals. Define the tasks you want to get done for the day.

- Daydream. Let your mind wander.
- Stay informed, not overwhelmed.
- Read a book.
- Do something different. Make a list of things you can do that are out of your normal routine.
- Help someone else.
- Have some fun.

Above all, remember these simple but powerfully insightful words:

"You don't have to have it all figured out to move forward. Just take the next step."
— Anonymous

It is true that we are in the middle of an unprecedented outbreak. But the sun will rise again, life does go on, and there are many tools to help us cope with stress.

Try to avoid catastrophic thinking, reflect often on all the good in your life, and above all, BREATHE.

You got this.

"LIFE IS LIKE RIDING A BICYCLE. TO KEEP YOUR BALANCE, YOU MUST KEEP MOVING."

— *Albert Einstein*

WORDS TO REPEAT:
Where my mind goes, my body will follow.

COVID-19 SELF-CARE KIT

By assembling a self-care kit, you can create a tangible tool that can help you during times of stress. Small, soothing items such as these can bring a sense of calm during unpredictable times because they offer comfort and familiarity and can help redirect your thoughts.

Your personal self-care kit does not have to be anything elaborate. It can be as simple or sophisticated as you would like. You can use items from around your house or you might want to include an extra-special item or two.

How to assemble:

Choose a box or container of some sort to fill with your personalized self-care items. See a list of suggested items below. Feel free to customize your kit with whatever brings you the most comfort and joy. If possible, include items that will appeal to the five senses of taste, touch, smell, sound, and sight.

- Sanitizer
- Soap
- Latex gloves
- Face mask
- Gum
- Mints
- Favorite hard candy or snacks
- Scented hand lotion
- Aromatherapy oil, sachet, or beads
- Special photos of loved ones or pets
- iPod and/or headphones for favorite music
- Favorite book or magazine
- Journal and pens
- Fidget toy or grounding item
- Tissues

- Tea
- Small candle
- A cozy blanket
- Fuzzy socks
- Stress ball
- Favorite DVD
- Small stuffed animal
- A list of affirmations
- Self-massage tools
- Crystals or stones